Mastering the Meaning of the Bible

Mastering

The

Meaning

of the

Bible

by

John L. McKenzie, S.J.

DIMENSION BOOKS
WILKES-BARRE, PENNSYLVANIA

First American Edition
Published by Dimension Books
Wilkes-Barre, Pa.

Library of Congress Catalog Card Number 66-27469

Grateful acknowledgment is hereby made to the following publications for permission to reprint in revised form articles which they originally published: to *Ave Maria* for "How to Read the Bible" and "Getting to Know Christ;" to *The Way* for "An Everlasting Love;" to *U.S. Catholic* for "Sex Is in the Bible;" to *The Catholic Mind* for "The Biblical Movement and the Laity;" and to *The Catholic World* for "The Bible in Contemporary Catholicism."

Contents

1. How to Read the Bible 7

2. An Everlasting Love 27

3. Getting to Know Christ 57

4. Sex Is in the Bible 77

5. The Bible in Contemporary Catholicism 97

6. The Biblical Movement and the Laity 119

How to Read the Bible

Reading the Bible is not as difficult as many think, but it would be dishonest to say that it is easy. The Bible is a very large book — it is, in fact, a library rather than a book; and the arrangement of its parts, when the reader first meets them, is disconcerting. If we begin to read it where we usually begin books, at the beginning, we are likely to feel lost before we get very far; if we persist, in spite of our uncertainty, we may feel not only lost, but bored. When this happens, the reader will probably give up the task as impossible, at least for him.

The first and most important step for any one who wishes to read the Bible seriously is to get a good modern translation.

Two important modern translations by Catholics are the Bible of Monsignor Ronald Knox and the Old Testament now being produced by the Confraternity of Christian Doctrine. My own preference is for the Confraternity version. It is written in modern English, it divides and arranges the text, it has illuminating marginal notes and footnotes, and it preserves the poetry of the Bible.

The Revised Standard Version, prepared by a group of Protestant scholars, is also a very good version. It is available in a Catholic edition which has a number of minor changes in the New Testament part only. Richard Cardinal Cushing has approved the unchanged RSV as found in the Oxford annotated Bible, a valuable volume for students.

Once a readable translation is secured, the next question is where to attack the Bible. You can begin with the beginning, although in my own classes I have for some years begun with Genesis 12 and postponed the first eleven chapters until the book of Genesis is read to the end.

But the reader should not attempt the discouraging task of reading the Bible from there to the end of the Apocalypse. He ought to read it in selections; then he can return to the omitted passages, most of which he will read with greater interest and understanding. There are some passages which need not be read at all. A list of recommended selections is found in **Foreword To The Old Testament,** by Father F. L. Moriarty, S. J., and the beginner would be well advised to follow some such list of suggested readings.

When you read the historical books of the Old Testament, it is extremely important to remember what the Pontifical Biblical Commission stated in 1948: that we do not have here history in the modern sense of the word, but history as the ancients conceived and wrote it.

Ancient history is the telling and later the writing down of the collective memory of a family, a clan, a tribe, and ultimately a nation. Quite often this collective memory is unable to reproduce the past exactly, and it turns to imaginative reconstruction where memory has failed. We find this kind of material in the Bible, and it should cause no apprehension that we do. In inspiring men to write the sacred books, God has accepted the literary forms in use among men.

This collective memory of the past, sometimes

11

called folklore or popular tradition, was the only way in which the memory of the past was preserved in the ancient world outside of official royal records or annals. These annals were kept in the Hebrew monarchy, but not earlier. In particular, we must not look for a documentary history of those events which are by definition pre-historic: events which belong to the beginnings of humanity and to persons of which there is no written record anywhere. This has special reference to the first eleven chapters of Genesis and to a lesser extent to the stories of the Hebrew patriarchs; these are family traditions, of the kind with which we are acquainted in our own families.

What we call the history of the Hebrews is not a continuous narrative. There are large gaps, sometimes of a century or more. The narrators were interested in those events which they considered important; and these are not always the events which a modern historian considers important. Wars, the foreign relations of the Hebrew people, the social and economic development of the Hebrews, are treated briefly. The interest of the narratives is religious, and the stories include historical material of this sort only as it touches religious interests.

And this leads us to the key not only of Hebrew history, but of the entire Bible: **it is the story of the encounter of God and man, of the way in which God has interposed Himself in history and forced men to attend to His reality and to His power and will in the government of the world and of the course of human history.**

If there is one thing we learn from the Old Testament, it is that this is a violent encounter; men set up a gigantic resistance to God's intervention by their refusal to recognize His living reality. This gives the history of the Hebrews its tragic character. Their refusal to recognize the reality of God and His moral will was responsible for their ultimate historical failure as a nation to survive, though there were of course some who did recognize the reality of God and thus preserved the faith which was present when God Himself came to the earth.

With the historical books you should also read

the prophets. The modern reader finds the prophets the least sympathetic books of the Bible. Here it is important to remember that these books are compilations, and in some parts they are mere fragments. These discourses and poems and fragments were delivered over an extended period of time. Older translations do not make this clear; modern versions, with their headlines and marginal notes, help us to see that we are not reading a continuous piece of writing.

Where possible we should relate each piece to its proper historical situation. Since this is rarely possible, we should acquaint ourselves with the historical and religious background against which the prophets spoke. There are some passages which are so obscure that the reader had better omit them the first time over. Familiarity with the entire Bible and with Hebrew history as well as collateral reading will be necessary before these passages become clear.

When we read the prophets, we must have some idea of who the prophet was and what he was trying to do. This is difficult, since there is nothing in our experience which corresponds precisely to the prophet's mission. The Church is the custodian of revealed doctrine and its only authorized teacher. In ancient Israel the priests were the custodians of Hebrew tradition and they also had the office of explaining it.

The prophets, too, appealed to tradition, but it was their office to apply the traditions to the existing historical situation. And this often meant that their words were revolutionary, as their understanding of God and Hebrew traditions was widened and deepened with the advance of history. They were spokesmen of the living God, and their charisma was "the word of the Lord;" through them He spoke to Israel in its crises.

The inspiration of the prophet and the psychological processes of receiving a divine communication are extremely complex and to a degree defy analysis. The prophets' knowledge of God was mystical, above the level of faith and reason. There is an obscurity in their descriptions of their own personal encounters with God which we cannot remove, and we must remember this when we read these words. We read the prophets as the spokesmen of God, and where their meaning is clear, as it usually is, they deserve our close attention.

It is impossible in this context to give a complete summary of what the prophets said, but we can point out a few things which the reader ought to look for. The most representative prophetic books are Amos, Hosea, Isaiah and Jeremiah.

The first of these is the prophetic conviction of God's reality and also of His nearness. God, Amos tells us, is actively interested in human history. This active interest takes the form of a will which moves history towards an end which God has determined. This term, in its simplest form, is salvation, deliverance from the evils which man has brought into the world by his own evil will.

The prophetic conviction of the vivid personal reality of God gives their words an overpowering moral earnestness. For the prophets what man does is serious and important, not only for himself and for his fellow men, but also for God. This is what gives human life whatever meaning and value it has, though most of the time the prophets seem to be less interested in the individual person than in the nation of Israel as a whole.

The modern idea of the dignity and importance of the individual person, which is really a Christian idea, is less prominent in the writings of the Old Testament. However, the nation of Israel is often conceived and addressed as an individual person, and this is extremely vivid in the prophets. The adventures of Israel with God represent the adventures of the individual person with God; and this is the lasting significance for us of both Old Testament prophecy and Old Testament history. Once this spiritual adventure of Israel with God is understood, we shall have no difficulty seeing our own spiritual adventure reflected in the story. The bad will, the weakness, and the sufferings of Israel are those of the individual person. They reveal the ways of God with man. On the basis of this revelation Jesus could later reveal these ways more profoundly.

A common misconception is that the prophets are mere foretellers of the future. If the prophets are read with this misconception, most of what they say must be understood by the reader as referring to the future, and it becomes so obscure to him that he can find in it no meaning and no value.

We must understand that the prophets spoke to a living audience of people as real as ourselves — people with political, social, economic, and personal problems. It was their primary purpose to tell these people how they could meet these problems and in meeting them find God. Naturally they had a view of the future; everyone does. The prophetic view of the future, reflected also in other Old Testament books, now goes by the name of messianism. It is a hope and a conviction that the problems of man, whether individual or social, will be solved only by an intervention of God which is outside and beyond purely historical forces.

We take a narrow view of the prophetic view of the future, and we render their words less inspiring, if we think that their insight into the future is limited to the prediction of a few details in the life of Jesus Christ. The tremendous revolutionary fact of the Incarnation was hidden from their view. But their vision of God's saving will was what prepared men to accept this revolutionary fact.

The wisdom of the Old Testament includes all books which are neither history nor prophecy, and thus it includes such ill-mated items as the Psalms, which is a collection of hymns and prayers, and the Song of Solomon, which is a collection of love lyrics. Proverbs, Job, Ecclesiastes (or Koheleth), the Wisdom of Solomon, and Ecclesiasticus (or Ben Sira) are the books of wisdom of the Old Testament. Wisdom meant skill in the management of one's life and affairs by which one could avoid trouble and secure the maximum of happiness.

At times we may find the wisdom of the sages uninspiring. Their morality may seem pedestrian, even utilitarian. But their affirmation that clean living will protect a man from evil has a universal validity. The sages could not believe that a man could be better off for doing evil.

The problem, of course, is more complicated

than that, and these complications are taken up in Job and Koheleth. These books are profound and hard to interpret. They are the Hebrew effort to wrestle with the problem of suffering, and we may think they are not very successful. We have to remember that we have not solved the problem ourselves, and that the New Testament teaches us only how to live with evil — not how to think about it.

The Gospels tell us that even God incarnate could not escape suffering, and that He did not overcome it except by submitting to it. This is substantially the position which Job reached. He learned that a new vision of God is reached through the discipline of suffering, and that suffering does not become tolerable until that new vision is attained.

Christians see in the Gospels the vision towards which Job struggled through an agony of pain and doubt. Koheleth is even less satisfactory, as far as understanding the problem is concerned. He is convinced of the vanity of human effort and human success, and he is sure that man cannot find in the world the fulfillment which his nature demands. But it is not despair, except of the world and of man; in the book as we have it, Koheleth is sure that the fulfillment which man seeks can be found in God. His refrain: "Vanity of vanities, and all is vanity" has long echoed in Christian renunciation; here as elsewhere the Old Testament prepares for the unworldliness of the Gospel.

Unlike the Old Testament, the New Testament can be and ought to be read entirely, and of course after the Old Testament; but it is not all equally easy. The simplicity and the grandeur of the Gospels rank them not only the greatest books of mankind, but also among the easiest to read. They are dominated by the personality of Jesus Christ, the incarnate Word, and there is nothing obscure or repellent about His personality.

All four evangelists wisely refused to attempt an exhaustive portrait of the God-Man. Each selected those features which he or the tradition he followed desired to emphasize. The Fourth Gospel is often called the most elevated or sublime, a designation which is slightly misleading;

but its difference from the other three in such points as the relations of Jesus and His Father, which are merely indicated in the other Gospels, must be noticed. The reader will be rewarded by his efforts to visualize the consistent personality which emerges from the four documents.

In reading the Acts and the Epistles we must remember that we are reading about the primitive Church. The identity between the primitive Church and the Church in which we live may be compared to the personal identity between the infant and the adult. It is the same person, although the external features can scarcely be recognized.

The apostles did not teach all the truths which the modern Church teaches. They possessed the Christian revelation as a child possesses his inheritance. He has it, but he does not yet know what is in it. The primitive Church does not exhibit the complex and closely knit organization of the modern Church. The sacramental discipline of the apostolic Church shows some striking differences; the Sacraments which are mentioned are the same Sacraments, but their administration is at times difficult to recognize. To see the inner identity of the primitive Church and the modern Church will give us an insight into what our Church really is — Jesus Christ living in His members.

The Epistles, especially the Epistles of St. Paul, contain some of the most difficult passages of the entire Bible. Many of these difficulties vanish if one knows the Old Testament well enough. Most of the first Christians were Jews, and St. Paul could address them in biblical language and employ biblical arguments.

At other times he appeals to Jewish traditions and Jewish interpretations with which the modern reader cannot become familiar without some specialized reading, for which he probably has neither the time nor the material.

Nowhere in the Epistles do we have a coherent and continuous exposition of doctrine. Such expositions were given in the primitive Church, but they are not preserved except in the Synoptic Gospels; for the principal part of the exposition was the story of the life and death of Jesus Christ.

When this teaching is expanded and applied, it issues in the dogmatic and moral parts of the Epistles.

The last book of the New Testament, the Apocalypse, is the most obscure of all biblical books, and no one who has tried to read it needs to be told this. But we can point out that it is a presentation of the same belief which we find in the prophets, the final victory of God over evil, and that it is described with a profusion of imagery drawn both from the Old Testament and from contemporary history, which is reflected in its pages. The reader must remember that he is dealing with one vast figure of speech, and that God's salvation and judgment are described in extremely poetic and often exaggerated terms. You can lose sight of the essential conviction if you are distracted by the luxuriant details.

A reader of the Bible should be assured that to a large extent the Bible explains itself. Familiarity with the entire text is the fundamental skill which the interpreter and teacher of the Bible needs; for this there is no substitute. Reading books and articles on the Bible and its background is of course also essential for the interpreter, but it is less necessary for the layman who wishes to read the Bible intelligently as well as devoutly.

Serious and planned reading of the Bible will give us more familiarity with biblical style and patterns of thought than we think possible. Once this is acquired, we can read the Bible with assurance and understanding. We will find the Bible spiritually enlightening and inspiring, as well as interesting and even thrilling too.

An Everlasting Love

Love — the love of God for man, of man for God and of man for man — is both the dominant pathos and the central moral theme of the New Testament. There is no book of the New Testament in which love is not mentioned, and the kind of love which is specifically christian was so much a novelty that to express its revolutionary significance, it was necessary to infuse new meaning into a Greek word rarely seen in profane literature.

The New Testament book in which it is said that God himself is love[1] is by common critical consent considered to be among the later writings of the New Testament: it is not merely fanciful to think that this insight came after a generation or two of reflection on the surpassing love of God for man, as revealed in Christ Jesus. God's love has become such a commonplace in christian life, worship and literature that we frequently forget how difficult it is to enter the mystery of this love. Love, when

1. Jn 4, 8

we speak of God's love, is as much an anthropomorphism as God's wrath or God's eyes. It is possibly the boldest of all the biblical images in which God is described in human traits.

Biblical scholarship has very nearly demolished the venerable falsehood that the Old Testament is the law of fear, and the New Testament the law of love. When Jesus uttered words like "Fear him who, after he has killed, has power to cast into hell,"[2] he was not proclaiming a dispensation of love unmixed with fear. Those, incidentally, who are apprehensive when the disciples seem to contradict the master will not be pleased when they compare the above text with this one: "There is no fear in love, but perfect love casts out fear; for fear has to do with punishment, and he who fears is not perfected in love."[3] Jesus in his life was obviously addressing those who had not achieved perfect love; one may indeed ask at what point perfect love can be expected. Nevertheless, John does present an ideal of perfect love which rises entirely above the level of fear; and this is uniquely a New Testament idea.

2. Lk 12, 5

3. 1 Jn 4, 1-19.

AN EVERLASTING LOVE

The false opposition between fear and love to which I referred above springs from a desire on the part of biblical writers to propose a truth which should never become obscure to us: the novelty of the revelation of the gospel. To maintain this truth and at the same time to maintain the continuity of Old Testament and New Testament can easily place the interpreter in a paradoxical position. The Gospel had to be proclaimed in some language; and by language we mean not merely the linguistic symbols but language in the larger sense as a medium of communication identified with a distinct historical and cultural group. The gospel was first proclaimed in the language of Judaism; preachers were anxious to show in what sense the christian mystery of God's love is both a development of the Old Testament and a departure from it.

No serious student of the Old Testament can think that Yahweh, the God of Israel, was a composite of the common beliefs of the ancient Near East. In every point of comparison he appears totally dissimilar to the gods of the ancient world.

At the same time, Israel was a member of the cultural community of the ancient Near East. The way in which Israel spoke of Yahweh was determined not only by Yahweh's revelation of Himself but also by the cultural heritage which Israel shared. Its manner of thinking and speaking of the deity was not as unique and incomparable as the deity of whom Israel thought and spoke. Not infrequently, one sees the prophets and sages of Israel struggling to express the mystery of Yahweh in concepts and language which they knew were inadequate for their purpose. At other times the Israelites were content to borrow language and images from their neighbors and apply them to Yahweh, especially where there was no clear contradiction between these borrowed images and the God whom they portrayed. For example, Yahweh, like a number of gods, was presented as the lord of the storm who makes the clouds his chariot and brandishes the thunderbolt as the weapon of his wrath.

In the ancient religious literature which we possess and which could have been known to

Israel there is no genuine idea of God's love. Generalizations such as this are too broad and they can be misleading; but this one does not distort reality too much. I am not concerned here with the conventional language of hymns and psalms, though even these do not have God's love as a theme. I speak rather of the concept of divine persons which we can synthesize from the literature of Mesopotamia, Canaan and Egypt. Love is not an attribute of these divinities. They are conceived as benevolent, even at times as friendly. They are conceived as capable of good deeds, of showing favor to men. But ultimately they are incapable of love, and the reason for this is rooted in the reality of which the gods of the ancient Near East were a personification. This reality is nature; the gods were not more capable of love than nature is capable of it. When the Israelites formed an idea of God's love, they did not and could not have formed it on anything they learned from their neighbors. That the idea does not appear in the earliest period of Israelite history should cause no surprise.

Yahweh does appear in characters which resemble the characters of the gods of Israel's neighbors and some of these deserve our attention. The
three characters which are most relevant to the
idea we are considering are the characters of king,
lord and father. These three overlap. The king is
the absolute and supreme head of the political
society. The lord is the owner of a household,
which includes the members of the household:
wife or wives, children, slaves. The father-figure is
not conceived in terms of the modern father of a
family; this qualification should be remembered
when the fatherhood of Yahweh is mentioned in
the bible. The idea does not always imply paternal
love, although in the Old Testament this idea is
frequently implied. The idea of paternal authority
is also implied, and in the religion of Israel's neighbors this is the dominant idea when the gods are
addressed as father. The king is called both lord
and father of his people; and the three figures
merge into an image of benevolent despotic power.
Not love but condescension is the determining
attribute. I believe it is not unimportant to em-

phasize these features of ancient Near Eastern belief, if we are to see clearly the theological pattern
from which Israelite belief broke.

The entire Old Testament echoes and re-echoes
the themes of the exodus and Sinai and the law.
It seems that the modern popular idea of Yahweh
as the God of Israel is drawn mostly from these
recurrent themes. Have not most of us learned to
think of the God of Israel primarily as the God of
Sinai, the lawgiver who appears in smoke and
flame, in thunder and earthquake? This impression
has been conveyed by the movies of the late Cecil
B. DeMille. Possibly his version of the exodus and
the covenant will be seen by more people than any
moving picture since **The Great Train Robbery.**
Certainly DeMille's version of the story has been
seen by millions who have never read the biblical
version. It may not be beside the point to notice
that DeMille's film, **The Ten Commandments,** falls
neatly into a literary category known as midrash.[1]
But with or without midrash, it must be granted
that the God of Sinai is not a figure who inspires

---

1 An Ancient Jewish, homiletic commentary on the scriptures making free use of allegory.

love. The earliest Israelite narratives describe the reaction of the Israelites themselves as sheer terror.

The recent studies of G. E. Mendenhall and others have made the biblical account of the covenant more intelligible. But they have not removed any of the terror. We can now identify the God of Sinai more precisely as a figure of the overlord who imposes his will on his vassals through a treaty of suzerainty. Obligations are imposed and sanctions are attached in these treaties. But the overlord commits himself to nothing. The promises attached to the covenant of Israel are far more generous and specific than the promise made by the ancient overlord to his vassals. But they are the promises of the overlord — again, not a figure who inspires love. It is curious that the ancient treaties contain the stipulation that the vassal is to "love" his overlord. This stipulation does not appear in the earliest Israelite law. Nothing is lost by its absence. The "love" imposed in the treaties of suzerainty is love in the technical sense of loyalty to the overlord and fidelity to the stipulations of the treaty. When the idea of love between God and man arose in Israel, it advanced far beyond this merely legal sense. It is more relevant to our purpose to note that while the vassal is obliged to love the overlord, love is not expressed by the overlord towards the vassal. Such love would be beneath the overlord; and here we have the problem in a nutshell.

These considerations are introduced because they show that God's love did not become known in Israel through a reasoning process. God's love was known only through his revelation of himself as loving. Whether it could have been reached by reasoning is a purely speculative point of interest. Among human beings love is not recognized by deduction but through intuition. The timidity with which this intuition begins has been the theme of countless poets and novelists. That another person feels love for one is an idea which at first seems too daring to be credible. But when genuine love exists, it reveals itself through compelling signs — not only words and deeds, but all the little movements which have a meaning all their own, to borrow a phrase from a somewhat vapid contemporary lyric.

The analogy between human and divine love breaks down at several points, of course. One point is the timidity with which human love is so often expressed in its initial stages. We have noticed that God's love is scarcely expressed in the earliest Israelite literature; when it is expressed, it is revealed with overwhelming vigor and fullness.

This first expression came in the prophecy of Hosea. The book of Hosea is to be dated in the second half of the eighth century B.C., some hundreds of years after the beginnings of Israel as a people. Hosea addressed Israel in the supreme crisis of its history, the crisis in which Israel ceased to exist as a distinct political society.

Elsewhere I have described the book of Hosea as a book of divine passion. The attribution of emotion to Yahweh is an Old Testament commonplace. Nowhere in the Old Testament is emotion attributed to Yahweh with so little restraint as in Hosea. Of all the loves in which the love of Yahweh for Israel could be conceived, Hosea prefers the love of man and woman; and he also conceives it as the love of the father for his children.

That this theme is original with him is not certain. But his expression of it deserves the term original if any literature deserves it. The love of man and woman, like the love of father and children, was not entirely the same in the ancient world as it is in the modern world. Under ancient law the woman was the property of the husband. The image of marriage could be used with no trace of affection.

Interpreters commonly associate Hosea's intuition of God's love with his own personal experience related in chapters 1 and 3. These autobiographical allusions are extremely obscure, and there is no agreed interpretation of them in all detail. But the general drift of the passages is clear enough for Hosea's message and shows that Hosea loved a wife who was unfaithful. Here our understanding is aided if we recall the attitude of the ancient world towards adultery. In ancient codes of law the normal punishment of the adulterous wife was death. Some codes provided for condonation by the husband; but it was the option of the husband to condone or to demand the full legal penalty. We have no way of knowing what the

practice was, but it is unlikely that the severity of
the law was out of harmony with public opinion
entirely. A more tolerant modern society does not
readily sympathize with the loathing which was
felt for adultery in the ancient Near East.

These indications suggest that Hosea's behavior
as he describes it was exceptional. He shows himself as a man so deeply and foolishly in love with
his wife that he cannot dismiss her even when she
is unfaithful. We can scarcely doubt that Hosea's
neighbors and contemporaries would regard him
as a very simple and unduly meek fellow. His love
is not so much forgiving as tolerant.

This attitude is not described without qualification. Hosea makes it clear that he was torn by con-
flicting emotions; a point can come where tolerance is no longer possible, where love yields to
anger.

This is the kind and condition of love which
Hosea attributes to Yahweh: tolerant, almost helpless in the face of unforgivable disloyalty, in ten-
sion with a mounting anger as love is rejected.
Indeed, once God's love is revealed in terms of

human feeling, Hosea could not but represent a conflict of emotions. History showed that tolerant love finally gave way to righteous anger, and Yahweh destroyed Israel.

Hosea is not simply the prophet of love any more than the Gospel is simply a message of love. But his book does break new ground. Hosea is the first Israelite on record to idealize the early period of Israelite history as a period of mutual love of Yahweh and Israel. He sees it as the honeymoon, the time of the passionate love of youth. The initiative of love came from Yahweh — a theme which elsewhere is called election. In the ancient world it was fitting that the wealthy husband should shower his wife with gifts; this Yahweh had done. To a modern reader this may sound as if Hosea thought love could be purchased. But Hosea was as well aware that this is false, as was the author of the Song of Songs.[1] Israel had responded to Yahweh's love with full devotion. It is this which makes Israel's infidelity so odious. It also heightens the anger of Yahweh. Hosea expresses the anger of Yahweh with the same flaming

1. Cant 8, 7

passion with which he speaks of love. The terrible threats of chapter 13 equal in their intensity anything in the prophetic literature.

This intense anger is not the result of a sudden impulse. The love of Yahweh is so deep that it inhibits his anger. Hosea does not hesitate to represent Yahweh as vacillating between tolerance and punishment, between love and anger:

> *How can I give you up, O Ephraim!*
> *How can I hand you over, O Israel!*
> *How can I make you like Admah!*
> *How can I treat you like Zebolim!*
> *My heart recoils within me,*
> *my compassion grows warm and tender.*
> *I will not execute my fierce anger,*
> *I will not again destroy Ephraim:*
> *For I am God and not man,*
> *the Holy One in your midst,*
> *and I will not come to destroy.*[1]

This vacillation disappears in chapter 13:

> *So I will be to them like a lion,*
> *like a leopard I will lurk beside the way.*

---

1. Hos 11, 8-9

I will fall upon them like a bear
  robbed of her cubs,
 I will tear open their breast,
and there I will devour them like a lion,
  as a wild beast would rend them.
I will destroy you, O Israel;
  who can help you? . . .
Shall I ransom them from the power of Sheol?
  Shall I redeem them from Death?
O Death, where are your plagues?
  O Sheol, where is your destruction?
Compassion is hid from my eyes.[2]

When I use the word vacillation to describe this
attitude, I am of course indulging in simplification.
Hosea does not represent the anger of Yahweh as
final. It is ultimately love which prevails. In chapter 2 the chastisements of anger are intended to
teach Israel that it needs the love of Yahweh to
live. The threats of chapter 13 yield to the quiet
invitation and promise of chapter 14. Critics have
questioned with some probability whether chapter
14 is the work of Hosea himself or of a continuator.

2. Hos 13, 7-9, 14.

Critical questions can be important for interpretation; here we can say that whether the lines come from Hosea or from another, they carry on the genuine thought and feeling of Hosea. How Yahweh's love is to find fulfillment, Hosea does not know. It is very probable that he wrote just before or during the collapse of the kingdom of Israel, and a restoration of Israel did not appear on the historical horizon. The book closes with a profession of faith in Yahweh's love, a love which is strong enough to realize itself even when history appears to leave no room for its realization. A love with such a past cannot be a love without a future.

The literary relations between Hosea and Deuteronomy are obscure. The earliest form of Deuteronomy is to be placed in the seventh century before Christ, less than a hundred years after Hosea. Deuteronomy reflects in several ways the traditions of Israel rather than of Judah; and Hosea was a man of Israel. It is probably not purely coincidental that only Deuteronomy of the traditions of law and covenant introduces the theme of Yahweh's love of Israel. Like Hosea, Deuteronomy is written in a tone of urgency which reflects the historical crisis created by the Assyrian empire. In such a crisis Israel and Judah could escape annihilation only by a response to Yahweh's love.

In Deuteronomy the theme of election is prominent, and this theme is found in other books also. But Deuteronomy makes election an act motivated by sheer preventing love. This love was first shown to the fathers of Israel.[1] Israel inherits this love not because it deserves it or has earned it by merit; but because it is the object of a gracious choice.

It was not because you were more in number than any other people that the Lord set his love upon you and chose you, for you were the fewest of all the peoples; but it is because the Lord loves you, and is keeping the oath which he swore to your fathers, that the Lord has brought you out with a mighty hand, and redeemed you from the house of bondage, from Pharaoh, King of Egypt.[2]

It is not surprising that Deuteronomy also emphasizes the duty of Israel to respond to the love of Yahweh. The book imposes on Israel not only

1 Deut 4, 37: to 15   2. Deut 7, 7-8

45

single loyalty and obedience, but loyalty and obedience rooted in love. A glance at the texts of the suzerainty treaties shows that the tone of Deuteronomy and the kind of love demanded here are entirely different from the technical "love" of the vassal given to the overlord. Jesus found in Deuteronomy the line which he said contained the greatest and the first commandment.[3] When he wished to propose the basic attitude of the christian way of life, he found this attitude expressed in the text of the Torah, the work which was regarded in Judaism as the one and sufficient means of salvation. Before man's love of God could become an effective reality, man had to learn that God loves him.

Just as the literary relations between Hosea and Deuteronomy are obscure, so are the relations between Deuteronomy and Jeremiah obscure. If we accept 622 B.C. as the date of the promulgation of Deuteronomy, as most critics do, then it is almost impossible to suppose that Jeremiah was unacquainted with Deuteronomy. But he may not have been acquainted with the introductory dis-

3 Deut 6, 5

46

courses, from which most of the passages cited are taken. It is also difficult to establish a certain dependence of Jeremiah on Hosea. A community of theme is evident beyond all doubt; for Jeremiah is a prophet of Yahweh's love of Israel, and a pathetic prophet.

Jeremiah resumes the theme of Israel as the faithless bride of Yahweh, particularly in the poem of chapter 2. Like Hosea, he idealizes the past of Israel, the youthful devotion and the bridal love.[1] His candor in describing the faithlessness of Israel goes beyond the language of Hosea; his desire to paint the crime in all its ugliness leads him to a frankness which is rather strong for modern and western tastes. His emphasis falls on Yahweh's love as love unrequited. The emotional conflict between love and anger appears again. Jeremiah also was a prophet of crisis, and in the supreme crisis he appeals to the supreme motive. If love is not answered, then anger must result.

Jeremiah despaired of historic Judah. He sees no response to Yahweh's love, and therefore no

1. Jer 2, 2

hope for the people whom he addresses. But despair of Judah is not despair of Yahweh's love. Yahweh's love is more powerful than the malice of Judah, and Yahweh's love will find its fulfillment in a future which is only dimly discerned. This fulfillment is the theme of the great poems of chapters 30-31. Some critics doubt that these poems are the work of Jeremiah himself. But no one can doubt that they carry on his spirit and his feeling.

Jeremiah sees Yahweh's love achieving in the restoration something which it did not achieve in the history of Israel. A love so deep cannot end in divorce.[2] The dreadful punishment of Judah is another exodus into the wilderness like the exodus from Egypt,[3] and Yahweh appears again in the wilderness. He does this because his love is everlasting and his faithfulness continues.[4] Jeremiah sees more clearly than Hosea that the punishment, the work of Yahweh's anger, is really the work of Yahweh's love. Unless he punishes, he cannot make Israel an object of love, cannot

2. Jer 3, 1-5   3. Jer 31, 2-3   4. Jer 31, 3.

save Israel from its own bad will. Yahweh's love is too strong to be frustrated even by the object of the love.

After the collapse of Judah and the dispersion of historic Israel as a political community, faith in Yahweh's love could not have survived unless it became faith in the redeeming love proclaimed by Jeremiah. The prophet of this faith was the unknown author of Isaiah 40-55, designated as Second Isaiah or Deutero-Isaiah. This work can be dated by historical allusions in the years 550-545 B.C. Cyrus of Persia, the conqueror who annexed the Babylonian Empire to his own domains, had already appeared, and the course of his victorious career could be perceived. He was thé instrument, the "servant" through whom Yahweh would restore Israel. The work of Yahweh's redeeming love was approaching completion, and second Isaiah was the spokesman of redeeming love within the little Israelite community which had survived the fall of Judah.

The prophet is commissioned to speak words of comfort and tenderness to Israel.[1] This is indeed

1. Isai 40, 1-2

the tone of his discourses. Yahweh reveals himself in his forgiving love. Israel will be re-established as it was once established in the exodus. Kings and nations and the whole course of history cannot prevent the love of Yahweh from accomplishing its purpose.

Fear not, for I have redeemed you;
   I have called you by name, you are mine.
When you pass through the waters,
      I will be with you;
   and through the rivers, they shall not
      overwhelm you;
When you walk through fire you shall
      not be burned;
   and the flame shall not consume you.
For I am the Lord your God,
   the Holy One of Israel, your Saviour.
I give Egypt as your ransom,
   Ethiopia and Seba in exchange for you,
Because you are precious in my eyes,
   and honored, and I love you,
I give men in exchange for you,

peoples in exchange for your life.
Fear not, for I am with you;
  I will bring your offspring from the east,
  and from the west I will gather you;
I will say to the north, Give up;
  and to the south, Do not withhold;
Bring my sons from afar,
  and my daughters from the end
    of the earth. . .[1]

The love of Yahweh falls with a peculiar affection on Zion, the city of his temple:

But Zion said, The Lord has forsaken me,
  my Lord has forgotten me.
Can a woman forget her suckling child,
  that she should have no compassion
    on the son of her womb?
Even these may forget,
  yet I will not forget you.
Behold, I have graven you on the palms
    of my hands;
  your walls are continually before me.

---

1. Isai 43, 1-6

Your builders outstrip your destroyers,
   and those who laid you waste go forth
      from you.
Lift up your eyes round about, and see;
   they all gather, they come to you.
As I live, says the Lord,
   you shall put them all on as an ornament,
   you shall bind them on as a bride does.[2]

The possibility of a divorce between Yahweh and his people is eliminated. Yahweh does not bestow his love and then withdraw it; he is not like a man whose love can be alienated.[3] Fidelity is an essential attribute of the love of Yahweh, the very attribute which was lacking in Israel's love.

The biblical books selected for mention here do not exhaust the Old Testament theme of Yahweh's love; but they are its clearest and most passionate expressions. We have not yet arrived at the love disclosed in the gospels; but it is love we meet and not some other sentiment. The reader of the Old Testament notices that Yahweh's love

2. Isai 49, 14-18   3. Isai 50, 1.

is directed to Israel exclusively, and he misses the breadth of the New Testament. This is a limitation of Old Testament revelation which affects other themes also. For this reason I have drawn attention to the lack of parallels to God's love in the Old Testament. The marvel is not that God's love was known as directed exclusively to Israel; the marvel is that it was known at all.

God's love is described in terms of human love; this means that the Old Testament uses the language of passionate feeling. The images most frequently chosen are derived from family life. Yahweh has the love of a husband for his wife, of a father for his children. It is rare that the love of friendship is mentioned, for friendship implies equality and mutual reliance. The images of both father and spouse are continued and fulfilled in the New Testament. The language is bold and totally unmetaphysical; but it brings forth the reality of God's love as no other language can. The philosophy of Epicurus carried to the limit the metaphysical idea of a cold, remote and uninterested deity. Effectively this philosophy removed any communication between the divine and the human. Judaism in its later phases did not escape the danger of a god who was too distant to be the subject or the object of love. Such a god was not proclaimed by the prophets. The risk of excessive familiarity was preferred to the risk of widening the distance between man and God. The prophets did not wish to preserve God's dignity at the cost of his love.

If God's love in the Old Testament can be summed up in a single idea, it is the idea of a love which overcomes refusal. It is a love of election and a love of forgiveness, a love which creates and which restores. It is a love which is incorruptible. Man cannot destroy the love of God because he cannot merit it; it is not within his control. It cannot be said of the Old Testament as a whole that love is the dominant theme in the Israelite experience of Yahweh, or that love is presented as the motivation of Yahweh's action in history. All that can be said is that some Old Testament writers approach this conception. The everlasting faithful love of Yahweh was in the mind of St. Paul when he met the problem[1] of Israel's last and decisive refusal to accept the love of God revealed in Christ Jesus. What he found in the Old Testament was more than a minimal foreshadowing. When Jesus proclaimed the Father as one who loves, he did not introduce a total stranger.

A NOTE

Some readers will wonder why I have not introduced the **Song of Songs** into this consideration, and I owe an explanation. The interpretation of the Song which sees it as an allegory of God's love of Israel is very ancient and appears even in prechristian judaism. Most christian expositions of the **Song** have treated this theme. Some recent biblical scholars, however, have presented persuasive arguments for the thesis that this is not the literal and primary meaning of the **Song.** I find these arguments convincing enough to omit the **Song** from consideration here. The love of man and woman as a parable of God's love of

1. Rom 9-11

Israel is a solid Old Testament theme, whether it is found in the **Song of Songs** or not.

I have no desire to impose this interpretation on those who are not as convinced as I. But a treatment of the **Song** as an allegory of divine love will be written much better by one who believes that the **Song** is such an allegory; and I prefer to leave this treatment to others.

Getting to Know Christ

St. Paul once wrote that although he had formerly known Christ according to the flesh, he now knew Him so no longer (2 Corinthians 5:16). The meaning of this puzzling statement has never been entirely clear to interpreters. For St. Paul, as far as we know, never had a personal meeting with Jesus during his earthly life.

Thus it is quite likely, as Father Lilly indicates in his translation of the verse, that to know Christ according to the flesh means to know Him "externally," to know His external appearance, His human features and character, without realizing His position as Son of God and Redeemer. In the verse which follows the one in question, St. Paul points out that any one who is in Christ is a new creature; failure to realize this newness is to know Christ merely according to the flesh.

The modern Catholic, on the contrary, often feels that he would like to know Christ a little better according to the flesh. His Faith has taught him the doctrines of the Incarnation and the Redemption, and he does not find it difficult to think of Jesus Christ according to these terms. But he sometimes feels the lack of knowledge of Jesus as a fellow human being.

The historical Jesus is divided from us by 2,000 years of recorded history which have wrought vast and sweeping changes in the human scene. Even if our knowledge of history is not very extensive, it is enough to make it clear that the world in which Jesus lived was another world as far as we are concerned. Against a completely unfamiliar background His figure moves quite dimly. The miracles recorded in the Gospel create about Him an atmosphere of wonder which does not resemble the world of our own experience; and our awareness of His holiness and divinity leads us to imagine Him walking about with the halo of Christian art. We may easily think that in His own world Jesus was a mysterious and elusive figure.

If you were to stroll through the great European

collections of art, you would see how the great artists of the Middle Ages and the Renaissance dealt with the reality of the historical Jesus. They painted Him in the external features which even in the Middle Ages had become traditional: the smooth young face with wavy hair and beard, the long flowing garments and the bare feet which they thought represented the garments of Gospel times. All the biblical characters likewise appear in these antiquated garments, and the halo appears on Jesus and all those whom Christians venerate as saints.

But the background of these paintings was contemporary to the painters. Jesus and His apostles walk through the streets of the Renaissance cities of Italy and Flanders or through the countrysides of Tuscany and Holland. The background figures which do not belong to the Gospel stories are represented in the costume worn at the time of the painting. In this art Jesus and the Gospel have left Palestine and the first century of the Christian era and moved into the cities and among the people of early modern Europe.

Such a transfer is not entirely illegitimate. Jesus is not merely a great historical figure whose work long outlives himself; in the Christian faith He is Jesus ever living, and the Church worships the living Christ, not the dead Christ. Hence the fundamental faith which led these painters to represent Gospel scenes in this manner is not due merely to their ignorance of the historical and cultural background which they ought to have put in their pictures were they attempting a purely representational art.

Yet, such art does not succeed for us in representing the historical Jesus. Were we to imitate this art, we would change the background to the background of our times. But the central figure would remain as remote as He is in Renaissance art.

No certain representation of the external appearance of Jesus has been preserved. The traditional countenance which appears in almost all Christian art cannot be traced back to the memory of those who knew Him. In some of the early Christian art of Rome, Jesus is represented in an

entirely different manner; the most striking difference is the absence of the beard.

The artists of the early Roman Church not only
made the background contemporary, but also
brought the central figures up to their own times.
Christian devotion has almost from the beginning
of Christianity felt the need of a visible representation of the Incarnate Word; and we on our part
certainly feel it today.

The historian can but shudder at most of the
representations which are circulated among Christians, even at some of the work of great artists.
He is sure that the soft pink Christs favored by so
many artists resemble no native of the eastern
Mediterranean countries in New Testament times.
He has no doubt that Jesus was a fine figure of a
man, as the saying goes; but he also fears that if
Jesus were to walk into a modern suburban church
with His swarthy complexion, His workingman's
hands, and the weathered skin of the outdoor man,
He would be shown the door or the police would
be summoned to pick up the dangerous-looking
vagabond. Knowledge of Christ according to the

flesh in the sense that we can recapture His personal appearance is beyond our grasp.

Biblical scholars are often asked by their friends to recommend some book or books which will make the humanity of Christ real to them. The biblical scholar will recommend with hesitation some titles which he knows are good, such as M.-J. Lagrange's **The Gospel of Jesus Christ,** or **Jesus Christ** by Fernand Prat, both big, two-volume works translated from the French, or the one-volume **Life of Christ** by Giuseppe Ricciotti.

But he recommends them with hesitation because he knows the inquirer will not find in these books what he is seeking. The composition of the life of Christ has now been an unachieved goal of biblical scholarship for over 100 years. With the rise of modern critical study of the Bible in the early 19th century, men began to think that with the tools of modern historical research it would be possible to recover the real historical Jesus by prying off the incrustation of faith and mythology which was overlaid upon this historical figure.

And so the lives of Christ in German, French,

English and other languages began to pour from the pens of scholars. The stream has not yet dried up, but I have been assured by some of my colleagues that more and more the feeling is growing that the writing of the definitive life of Christ is an impossible goal. It is not without irony that we notice that each of those who wrote the life of Christ, with some few exceptions, thought that he had succeeded in writing the definitive life of Christ where his predecessors had failed.

They all failed because the definitive life of Christ has already been written. It is found in the four Gospels, and anyone who wishes to know Jesus as a genuine human being must go to the Gospels; ultimately the scholars who attempt to write His life have no other source on which to draw.

But the reader who opens the Gospels is immediately aware of two serious obstacles to understanding. The first is the strange world of the Gospels, which lies in a distant country and a remote century. If one wishes to overcome this barrier one must do some reading, and the books which I have mentioned above are excellent for the purpose. To some degree one must grasp that the difference in manners which we notice in the people of the Gospels are much less significant than the community we have with them. These people felt the same human needs, they had to pursue the same occupation of supporting themselves and their family, and they knew many of the menaces to their peace and security which are so familiar to us. It is not so difficult to realize this community as we might think.

The second obstacle is the language of the older translations of the Bible. Our Rheims New Testament, for example, was not a very good specimen of contemporary late 16th century English when it was first published because the translators employed far more unfamiliar words of Latin derivation than appeared in the common speech of the time. Subsequent revisions of the Rheims New Testament have removed many of these. But the language, simply because it is old, sounds stilted to modern ears, and it is extremely difficult to feel community when the speech of the people in the story sounds more like the declamations of Hamlet and Macbeth than like the speech which we hear on the streets, in stores and shops, in our homes.

The stilted character of the English Bible is all the more damaging because the Greek of the New Testament is not the Greek of the poet, philosopher, and orator, but the speech of the man in the street — the artisan, the shopkeeper. It is the true common language. Very few translations have succeeded in reproducing its "common" quality. We are fortunate that we now have the Gospels as translated by the late Father Kleist **(The New Testament,** translated by James A. Kleist, S.J., and Joseph L. Lilly, C.M., Bruce, Milwaukee, 1956). It is generally agreed that this translation, however it may be criticized for other reasons, is the most radical attempt to make the New Testament speak the English of the modern American; and it is also a very faithful rendition of the New Testament.

Readers of this version have told me that read-

ing the Gospels of Father Kleist's version was almost like reading them for the first time; they
were startled to find that Jesus and His apostles
could speak a language they could understand,
and this alone gave them deeper insight into the
Gospels.

With this tool it should be easier to read the
Gospels and to seek from them the revelation of
the genuine humanity of Jesus, which they do
contain. For if one reads the Gospels attentively,
there is scarcely a page in which this humanity
does not emerge. I shall mention merely a few of
many instances.

Jesus was one of the long line of small boys who
ran away to explore the great world without the
knowledge and consent of His parents (Luke
2:41 ff). To Him, as to us, sin was presented as an
alluring, desirable thing (Matthew 4:1 ff; Mark
1:12 ff; Luke 4:1 ff); and His community with us
in temptation should not be lost because the part
of the personal devil in His story lies outside our
experience. Life in a Palestinian village — and

anyone who has lived in a village anywhere knows this — has all the privacy of a goldfish bowl; and Jesus was thoroughly known to His neighbors, as they thought. They knew not only Him but also His whole family (Matthew 13:54 ff; Mark 6:1 ff; Luke 4:16 ff).

We can see that, as so often happens among us, His neighbors refused to believe that He was capable of rising above their level. Mediocrity punishes greatness for its mere existence. The narrative, however, reveals that Jesus was in no way withdrawn from the life of the village in which He lived; He plunged into it so deeply that His neighbors, among whom He had lived and grown to maturity, simply refused to believe that He had any unusual gifts or was capable of any unusual achievement.

We see Him as a guest at dinner: in the house of Peter's mother-in-law (Matthew 8:15; Mark 1:31; Luke 4:39), with a Pharisee (Luke 7:36 ff), with Martha and Mary (Luke 10:38 ff), and at a wedding feast (John 2:1 ff). There is nothing to indicate that Jesus was the kind of guest who frightened other guests; people were not afraid to entertain Him, because they never thought He was too good for them.

The Gospels tell us that He could be surprised (Matthew 8:10; Mark 6:6). He could show compassion for misfortune (Matthew 9:36; Mark 6:34; Matthew 15:32; Mark 8:2). Once He is said to have shown anger (Mark 3:5) and once impatience (Mark 8:12); and there are other incidents in which, although He is not said to show anger, His words and His actions indicate some degree of feeling. He could speak of Herod as a fox (Luke 13:32) and He was capable of quite severe language, which we find often enough, particularly in His great invective against the Pharisees (Matthew 23:1 ff).

He certainly did not frighten small children (Matthew 19:13 ff; Mark 10:13 ff; Luke 18:15 ff), and the picture of Jesus surrounded by small children who climb all over His person without fear or shame has been a favorite with Christian artists; in this instance they have succeeded in catching the reality of the scene, whatever the background may be.

He was capable of personal affection; He looked at the rich young man and liked Him (Mark 10:21), and Martha and Mary appealed for assistance when their brother Lazarus was ill because Jesus loved him (John 11:3). He was not only capable of appreciating humor but of bringing out the humor in a scene, as when He brought Zacchaeus down out of the tree to invite Himself to the home of Zacchaeus for dinner (Luke 19:1 ff). Some critics who have noticed that the Gospels never tell us that Jesus laughed have failed to notice that the word is used only once or twice of anyone and have drawn unwarranted conclusions about the seriousness of His demeanor.

Those who have traveled in the Near East will recognize in the expulsion of the money changers from the Temple (Matthew 21:2 ff; Mark 11:15 ff; Luke 19:45 ff) one of the rather typical rows which one observes so often in the streets of eastern cities; and these rows are usually more amusing than damaging. Certainly one who has dealt with the Oriental money changer will never again read this passage with the same indifference with which he used to read it.

Jesus could weep; He wept over jerusalem (Luke 19:41) because of the disaster which He foresaw for it, and He shared the grief of Martha and Mary at the tomb of Lazarus. Indeed, the writer says not only that He wept, but that He was deeply agitated (John 11:33-35). He felt fatigue and thirst (John 4:6) and hunger (Matthew 4:2; Luke 4:2). You will scarcely find a more human scene than the conversation of Jesus and the Samaritan woman at the well (John 4:6 ff), which is one illustration of something fairly typical in the life of Jesus: the easy exchange which anyone could have with Him. He was at all times accessible; and this accessibility is not gained by forbidding demeanor and by withdrawing oneself from common associations. And finally, His genuine humanity appears at no point so clearly as at that point when, like any one of us, He exhibited fear and anguish at the prospect of imminent pain (Matthew 26:36 ff; Mark 14:32 ff; Luke 22:40 ff) and begged that He might be delivered.

These instances are but a selection of samples of what runs through the Gospels. In addition, one may note that Jesus was altogether familiar with the little world in which He lived.

He had an eye for the wild flowers which bloom in such abundance in the meadows of Palestine after the winter rains (Matthew 6:28). He noticed the peasant planting his crops (Matthew 13:1; Mark 4:1; Luke 8:4). He had seen the women baking the daily bread for the household (Matthew 13:33; Luke 13:21). He watched the fishermen by the shore of the Sea of Galilee (Matthew 13:47) and the herdsmen whom one could see then as one sees them now in the hill country (Matthew 18:10 ff; Luke 15:3 ff), and from these herdsmen He drew the immortal picture of Himself as the good shepherd (John 10:11).

He was familiar with Palestinian roads and their dangers, and from them He created the parable of the good Samaritan (Luke 10:30 ff). He saw the beggars who infested the streets and the roads, as they still do (Luke 16:19 ff), and He felt deep compassion for them. He saw, as one may still see them, men standing in the streets waiting to be hired as casual workers (Matthew 20:1 ff). He drew on the familiar wedding scene for one of His most incisive parables, that of the wise and foolish bridesmaids (Matthew 25:1 ff).

Such touches as this, such keen observation of the daily activities of little people, are the touches which we admire in literature. Such observations we attribute to genius, and it gives literature a unique realism; this gift Jesus had. Not only could He see these things, but He could make them significant. The parables are not drawn from learning; they come from the scenes familiar to each of His listeners. These things brought His teaching down to earth and made it intelligible to the simplest. One who so mastered the common touch, who could speak so fluently to children, to the ignorant and slow-witted, was in no way remote from His surroundings.

If you seek a knowledge of Jesus as a real fellow human being, the Gospels give us more of this than history records of its great men. These touches have always been there, but readers do not always attend to them.

Even so, there are certain limits to our knowledge. The Gospels are an objective report; they
tell us what could be seen and heard. There is
none of the mind-reading, none of the interpretation of motives which are so dear to the modern
novelist. This is Jesus as He looked, as He sound-
ed. The personality is never grasped except by
its external manifestation. But Jesus was not the
kind of person who wears His heart on His sleeve;
He was not the extrovert who reveals the inner-
most depths of his mind and heart to any casual
acquaintance.

Such revelation is a sign of shallowness, and
Jesus was deep. There is in Him a certain reserve.
This reserve was combined with the greatest accessibility and friendliness; but those who dealt
with Him most closely were aware that He always
kept something in reserve. Human feelings He had
and He revealed them, but they noticed that His
feelings, unlike theirs, were always under control.
He had a dignity and a mastery which are not typ-

ical. But whatever His reserve, His words and His demeanor were always genuine and sincere; He had no need of deviousness or diplomacy.

There is one final step, which does not belong to biblical study, and it is with hesitation that I write of it. Christian mysticism has always been a search for a personal knowledge of Jesus; and the mystics are as one in telling us that He discloses Himself to those who seek Him. It is not my place here to discuss how this happens; but it is clear that one must do more than read the records of the life of Jesus.

You must also seek Him directly in prayer, convinced that He is no less accessible and friendly now than He is shown to be in the Gospels. You may expect from Him at least the minimum of civility; if one speaks to Him, He will answer.

Sex Is in the Bible

No student of history will say that our modern age is more preoccupied with sex than earlier ages. The fascinating mystery of sex has attracted and interested man from the beginnings of recorded history, and without doubt before our earliest records. In earlier times this interest has shown deviations and excesses unknown to modern society. But the practicing Catholic of our day is often uneasy about his responsibilities. He is aware that most of his contemporaries seem to regard sex purely as an instrument of joy to be employed according to the personal desires and convenience of the individual. He sees all around him the sanctity of marriage attacked by freedom of divorce and by a sometimes very casual attitude towards adultery and pre-marital sex relations.

The contrasts between the ideal of Christian sexual purity, which appears quite rigid to the modern world, and the easy loose behavior of so many of his neighbors makes it clear to him, more than anything else, how different is his life as a Catholic from the life of others. Scarcely an hour of the day passes when he is not reminded of this difference by some association with his friends, by his reading, by his entertainment. There are times when he feels a stranger in the world, and perhaps he thinks that the ancient monks of the desert were right in fleeing this moral jungle instead of attempting to live in it as practicing Christians. But this he cannot do, because he has responsibilities. Some one, he knows, must maintain the standards of Christian morality in the world, and the layman realizes that it is he and others like him who must do it.

Rarely, I believe, does our Catholic turn to his Bible for light and assistance in carrying this burden. If he does, he is astonished that this subject, which bulks so large in his own conscience, is mentioned so rarely in the New Testament.

What vague memories he has of the Old Testament probably recall no more to his mind than the fact that in the Old Testament its heroes were men who by some marvelous divine dispensation were permitted the privilege of polygamy. He may have a secret suspicion that the male animal is naturally and instinctively polygamous; and he does not wish to have this suspicion confirmed from the Bible, of all places.

Besides this, he may remember a few lurid episodes in which violent lust is portrayed, the episodes which have furnished the subjects for moving pictures, such as the stories of **David and Bathsheba** or **Samson and Delilah.** Both of these heroes, if he takes out his Bible to read about them, were endowed with a vigorous and inclusive sexual appetite which they satisfied with little restraint. Here certainly, he feels, there is no inspiration to lead the kind of life which as a Catholic he believes he must lead. And so he will not count the word of God among the means which will assist him to do his duty.

There is in the Bible a great deal more about the relations of man and woman than the stories of polygamous patriarchs and adulterous kings. We read, for instance, in the words of the wise men of Israel such lines as this: "He who finds a wife finds happiness: it is a favor he receives from the Lord" (Proverbs 18:22); and "Home and possessions are an inheritance from parents: but a prudent wife is from the Lord" (Proverb 19:14); and, even more frankly, "Have joy of the wife of your youth, your lovely hind, your graceful doe. Her love will invigorate you always: through her love you will flourish continually" (Proverbs 5:18-19).

Ben Sira advises, "Happy is the husband of a good wife; twice lengthened are his days. A worthy wife brings joy to her husband; peaceful and full is his life. A good wife is a generous gift bestowed upon him who fears the Lord" (Sirach 26:1-3). And these words are not without tenderness: "A woman's beauty makes her husband's face light up; for it surpasses all else that charms the eye. And if besides that her speech is kindly, his lot is beyond that of mortal men. A wife is her husband's richest treasure, a helpmate, a steadying column. A vineyard without a hedge is overrun; a man with no wife becomes a homeless wanderer" (Sirach 36:22-25).

SEX IS IN THE BIBLE

The pessimist Koheleth finds marriage among life's few comforts. "Enjoy life with the wife whom you love, all the days of your fleeting life under the sun" (Ecclesiastes 9:9).

Nor is the Bible without its love stories. The wooing of Rebecca (Genesis 24), the stories of Ruth and Boaz (Ruth 3-4) and of Tobias and Sarah (Tobias 7-8), while they exhibit the historical and cultural differences which divide us from the ancient Israelites, are nevertheless in their own proper context touching stories of how boy meets girl. And it is clear in such stories that we are not dealing with the relations of the sexes either as a matter of unrestrained passion or as the cold business of a marriage contract signed by the parents. Even the grim laws of the Hebrews provided that young love should not be divided by war: "Is there any one who has betrothed a woman and not yet taken her as his wife? Let him return home lest he die in battle and another take her as his wife" (Deuteronomy 20:7). Those who could cherish such a law would scarcely agree with Lovelace's line, "I could not love thee, dear, so much loved I not honor more." Here as so often in their literature the ancient Hebrews could be extremely realistic.

The Bible has its own account of the origins of sex. It is, if you permit the term, a theological reconstruction and not a scientific investigation. We read in Genesis 2 that the man was created first. All the animals were brought before him that he might give them a name, that is, that he might determine what they were and what was their place in the scheme of things.

Among them man found none that was fit to be his own companion. Then "the Lord God cast the man into a deep sleep, and while he slept took one of his ribs and closed up its place with flesh. And the rib which the Lord God took from the man He made into a woman and brought her to him. And the man said: 'She now is bone of my bone and flesh of my flesh. She shall be called Woman, for from Man she has been taken.' For this reason a man leaves father and mother and clings to his wife, and the two become one flesh" (Genesis 2:21-24).

This is not a biological explanation of the difference of the sexes, but an explanation of the institution of sex as it ought to be. Woman was created to be the helper of man, his companion and associate on equal terms — not the drudge and the prostitute of ancient Semitic civilization. Between man and woman there is a close natural attraction, for they are of the same species, of one bone and one flesh. Because of the love a man feels for a woman he abandons his own family to found another, and in this foundation he finds a union in one flesh with the woman which is the most intimate of all human associations.

This is sex in Hebrew tradition in its primitive institution: it was not sex as they knew it in the world of experience. In that world the relation of the sexes is a fall from its original integrity. This noble conception of the meaning of sex runs through the entire Old Testament. The ancient Israelites too lived in a world which was preoccupied with sex and sexual aberrations. Against this perversion Hebrew belief took a strong stand by referring sex back to its original purpose.

The difference of the sexes exists that the two may complement each other in the permanent institution of marriage. Only in this institution is sex reasonable. The cultivation of man's sexual powers in any other manner and for any other purpose is bound to lead to unhappiness, as the ancient Hebrew story tells us in Genesis 3. That a man should leave his father and mother and cling to his wife and that the two should become one flesh — this in Hebrew belief was the fulfillment of the sexes and the only basis for a secure and happy relation between them. On this basis rested in turn the security of the larger units of human society.

The Bible pays human love its highest tribute when it makes human love the type of the love of God and man. A commonly used formula of the covenant relationship between God and Israel, "You shall be my people and I will be your God," possibly imitates the formula of the marriage contract as we find it in some ancient documents: "She is my wife and I am her husband this day and forever."

The prophet Hosea, in a passage of delicate

human feeling, represents God addressing Israel as a faithless wife; and God appeals to the love with which He and Israel were first pledged to each other: "Therefore behold I will allure her and bring her into the wilderness and speak tenderly to her . . . And there she shall answer as in the days of her youth, as at the time when she came out of the land of Egypt" (Hosea 2:14-15). The image is repeated by Jeremiah: "I remember the devotion of your youth, your love as a bride" (Jeremiah 2:2), and by Ezekiel in a lengthy parable of unusual frankness: "I plighted my troth to you and entered into a covenant with you, says the Lord God, and you became mine" (Ezekiel 16:8).

This image is resumed in the New Testament. Jesus compares himself to the bridegroom (Mark 2:19), and the same comparison is attributed to John the Baptist, whose own joy is like the joy of the best man when he catches the voice of the bridegroom (John 3:29). St. Paul wrote to the Corinthians: "I betrothed you to one spouse, that I might present you as a chaste virgin to Christ" (2 Corinthians 11:2), and the seer of the Apocalypse beheld the holy city, the New Jerusalem, coming down from heaven as a bride adorned for her husband (Apocalypse 21:2). The love of Christ for the Church is the ideal of the love of husband for their wives (Ephesians 5:25-30).

Surely that relationship which is the figure of the highest and greatest spiritual reality is not itself considered in the Bible as something low and unworthy. Rather one would think that the Bible, presenting to us this noble reality, adopts the noblest love known to human experienece that we may in it grasp something of the unsearchable love of God.

This is the background against which we must read the **Song of Songs,** or the **Song of Solomon.** This book, which is to all appearances a collection of love lyrics, has a long and complicated history of interpretation. Even early Jewish interpreters took the book primarily as an allegory; that is, the human love of which the poet sings is not itself the object of his intentions, but is purely and simply an image of the love of God for Israel. This allegorical interpretation has been pursued by

Christian interpreters from earliest times, and it is still maintained by many modern scholars. It seemed that it was necessary to find some allegorical meaning in the book, or at least some meaning other than the expression of human love, because these interpreters thought that the expression of such sentiments was unworthy of a sacred and inspired book, the word of God.

The allegorical interpretation, however, has always been somewhat difficult. We have no other instance in the entire Bible, and indeed scarcely any in all literature, of an allegory which does not at some point identify itself for what it is. Without such an explanation the reader would be misled.

The opinion is growing among modern Catholic scholars that it is not necessary to find such an allegorical interpretation in the Song of Songs. Recent writers have proposed that we perhaps speak too poorly of human love if we say it is unworthy of the sacred books. They remind us that human love is viewed in the Bible as holy, although it is not, strictly speaking, a religious institution. At the same time it is a divine institution with a high moral purpose. As the basis of such important things as the family, domestic peace and harmony, and as inextricably linked with the personal happiness of those who enter it, it has great religious significance. The Bible frankly deals with human love as a thing good and proper. It sees in the desire of man and woman for each other which ultimately leads to the matrimonial union nothing unworthy of the human being.

Hence the Bible is not afraid to express the joys of human love as it does in the **Song of Songs.** For love is the natural relation of man and woman. It is of its nature a joyful union, and God desires that man should find joy in it. Neither in the faith of Israel nor in the Catholic faith is human love a purely secular and profane affair. Were it such, were it unworthy of the author of the sacred books, it would also seem unworthy to be elevated to the dignity of a sacrament. For matrimony consists in the contract, the pledge of love exchanged by the contracting parties. This consent becomes the means of grace for the parties.

One must concede that the expression of human

love and its joy in the **Song of Songs** is more frank
and earthy than we permit in modern polite society. This feature is not peculiar to the **Song of
Songs.** The entire Bible, Old Testament and New,
reflects differences in manners. We must draw a
distinction, which is not always easy, between
manners and morals. What is improper to us often
had no impropriety in ancient Hebrew society. One
must examine these differences to see whether
there is any moral issue involved. Quite often there
is no moral issue whatever in the fact that one
society does things in a way which is rejected by
another.

Generally speaking, the Bible, and in particular
the Old Testament, when it deals with vital processes and human relations, expresses the manners of the simple and in some ways primitive
society in which it arose. At first glance their manners may appear crude and offensive, and in us
they would be; but beneath the manners the basic
human desires, relationships and duties are unchanged. The Hebrews, like many simple people
in more modern times, spoke of the relations of the

sexes with unabashed frankness. We must remember that they belonged to a pastoral agricultural society in which privacy was a luxury enjoyed by no one.

Our own manners do not permit this: but we cannot read the **Song of Songs** unless we are willing to show some tolerance for Hebrew manners and style. So read, I think we shall find that the book expresses the true beauty of human love. It will help us if we remember that were human love not the passionate attachment which it is, it would have been a very weak image of the love of God and man. That which the Hebrews experienced in the relations of the sexes they believed a man should experience in his relations with God. The love of God was not a cold rational acceptance of the goodness of God, but an intensely felt desire of union with God, whom they recognized as a person and from whom they expected a personal response.

Modern Catholics often feel themselves distended between two opposite poles. The one pole is the dedicated cultivation of pleasure which is professed by so many of our contemporaries.

Pleasure is the supreme standard of judgment in human activities. Unfortunately, in a culture whose prosperity depends so much on a large and rapid turnover of manufactured articles, we are bombarded by advertising which urges us to live it up, to let no pleasure which our manufacturers offer us pass us by, to spend on joys and thus to avert the danger of economic depression. With this cult of the agreeable certainly goes devotion to the goddess of sex. The Bible does not deny that sex is agreeable; but it rejected a heresy already ancient in its days that sex was a goddess to be worshipped and served without any reference to the responsibilities which accompany man's sexual powers.

The other pole is puritanism. While the name is derived from the earliest Protestant settlers of North America, that which the name signifies is found nowadays perhaps as commonly among Catholics as among Protestants. Puritanism is a revulsion against the excessive cult of pleasure; and any Christian must feel some revulsion against the hedonism of the modern world. But just as the hedonist cultivates pleasure for its own sake, so the puritan believes that pleasure is evil in itself. And of all pleasures which man should withhold from himself, the pleasures of sex are the keenest and therefore the most dangerous and to be most sternly rejected. Puritans accepted the necessity of marriage, but as good Christians they were sure that no one should ever really enjoy it.

Now this puritanism is not the biblical view, nor is it the genuine Christian view. Christian asceticism, which for a higher purpose denies self and many of the pleasures of life, never affirmed that pleasure is evil in itself. In denying pleasure it affirms that the pleasure is good and is rejected, or rather exchanged for a higher good which cannot be obtained otherwise.

The biblical view of sex stands squarely between these two poles. It is healthy, clean and natural, neither worshipping pleasure nor fearing it. It accepts nature as God has designed it; admitting that man is fallen from his primitive ideal, it nevertheless believes that the institutions of nature are not themselves perverted by man's misuse of them, and that they are to be accepted in their total reality.

Possibly we moderns can learn something from the biblical view of the relations of man and woman. The attraction of the sexes for each other is a fact which no puritan belief or practice can ever eradicate. This attraction is the basis of the love which arises between the individual man and the individual woman, and this love in turn is consecrated in the matrimonial union. It is the Catholic view of life that human love is a vocation, and furthermore that all but a few members of the Church have this vocation rather than the vocation to the celibate life. They must in some way find their happiness here and in the world to come in the vocation of human love. In that love and by that love they will ultimately achieve their supreme destiny. With this imperative urging them, Catholics will not misunderstand the true nature of love if they think of it in the terms found in the inspired word of God.

The Bible in Contemporary Catholicism

During my seminary studies my religious superiors manifested their intention to assign me to teach the Bible. My fellow students who were aware of this regarded me with compassion; in their minds the study and teaching of the Bible was a dead end, which was most unlikely to afford me or anyone else the opportunity to arouse any interest or exercise any influence.

I saw at the time no reason to question this fraternal compassion except a vague hope that things which were so unfavorably situated could scarcely move in any direction but up. It is still something of a surprise to recall that I have lived long enough to see the Bible become an object of intense interest, a common topic of discussion on the social level, a sure attraction for lectures, magazine articles and books. I had the good fortune to begin my teaching of the Bible in 1943; this was the year of the encyclical **Divino Afflante Spiritu,** on the promotion of biblical studies.

It is not entirely correct to say that this document initiated what is called the biblical movement; the direction in which interpretation had been tending for at least a decade was already set. The importance of the encyclical lay in its recognition of this direction and its approval by describing the procedures of contemporary interpretation as the procedures which the Holy See wished biblical studies to follow. The biblical movement as a popular phenomenon did not follow the encyclical immediately; there were a few matters like war and reconstruction which hogged popular attention in 1943 and for the next few years. But the biblical movement seized popular attention in Europe shortly after the end of hostilities; this seems remarkable until one examines the reasons why the biblical movement caught the minds of so many.

Among these reasons I would include primarily the upheavals of the war itself. War always destroys, it never builds, and it leaves vacuums in the mind as well as ruins in cities. After a war people are dissatisfied with the prewar thinking which they blame for precipitating or for not averting the catastrophe; and among the victims of postwar dissatisfaction were religion and theology. Many thought religion and theology had been as helpless in the face of evil as the secular systems of thinking had been. Some simply rejected them, others with deeper faith thought they had failed in vitality and immediacy and needed revival rather than replacement.

And where should they look except in that theological source which had received the least attention in earlier theology and preaching? It happened that the biblical movement was there with some new principles and techniques of interpretation and a more articulate if still somewhat primitive statement of the theological meaning of the Bible. Demand met supply. Because the upheaval of the war was less catastrophic in the United States than it was in Europe, the biblical movement proceeded more slowly here.

It is difficult to sum up the biblical movement in

a few words; and no single summary of what it is has been written which describes it better than **Divino Afflante Spiritu.** For the present let us reflect briefly on the fact that the movement and the encyclical which describes it are explicit repudiations of Fundamentalism.

It would be unfair to Protestant interpreters, a number of whom have honored me by their friendship, to call Fundamentalism a Protestant attitude; it is interconfessional. But Fundamentalism has been and is strongest and most vocal in those Protestant denominations which have their largest following in the remote and least advanced parts of the United States, and which can be characterized as revivalist. One may suspect the implication here that Fundamentalism is most sympathetic to those groups which are least educated; this is exactly the implication which I wish to convey. To see if such a harsh judgment is based on fact, let us see if we can define Fundamentalism.

It is fair to say that Fundamentalism is difficult to define, because it is not a consistent, reasoned position. It could be called simply the conviction that the Bible means exactly what it says, and many of its supporters would define it thus; but it is not that simple. Modern scholars would define their own conviction in the same terms.

Fundamentalism implies certain prejudices in the methods of determining what the Bible says. It denies that the interpretation of the Bible can be a specialized skill, and that learning improves a man's qualifications to interpret the Bible. It affirms that any believing Christian with the English Bible in his hands is not only as well prepared to interpret the Bible as the scholar, but that he is better prepared. All the interpreter needs to know is the Bible — in the vernacular. Fundamentalism denies that it is possible for the believer to misinterpret the Bible, to misunderstand it because of differences in history and culture which divide him from the writers of the Bible.

The study of languages, of history, of archaeology have nothing to contribute to the study of the Bible except fringe values; their most notable contribution is to confirm the interpretation of which the believer is already certain. If they fail to confirm it or still worse raise questions about it, then they are damned as pure rationalism, liberalism or modernism. Fundamentalism will hear nothing of differences in patterns of thought and language, of different conceptions of history, of prescientific and prephilosophical thinking. Fundamentalism knows it all and has nothing to learn.

The Biblical movement and the encyclical have, I say, explicitly repudiated Fundamentalism; the program of biblical studies outlined by the Holy Father is opposed to Fundamentalism point by point, which will appear from a simple enumeration of some of the features of the program.

The interpreter must acquire facility in the original languages of the text (FOUR GREAT ENCYCLICALS OF POPE PIUS XII, Paulist Press, pp. 71-72), whereas the Fundamentalist refuses to believe that the existing translation ever needs correction, or that reference to the original can provide deeper understanding. The interpreter must employ a critical text (pp. 72-73), but the Fundamentalist regards textual criticism as an irreverent tampering with the word of God.

The interpreter of today has special tasks, because earlier interpreters failed to explain many questions, and were quite unaware of new problems which have arisen from our more profound knowledge of antiquity; and the Holy Father calls erroneous the belief that modern interpreters have nothing to add to earlier scholarship (pp. 77-78). The Fundamentalist reposes on what he calls "the traditional interpretation of the Church" with aggressive confidence and labels any abandonment of "traditional interpretation" as rash, scandalous and offensive to pious ears.

The interpreter must know that the literal meaning of a passage is not as obvious in ancient Near Eastern documents as it is in modern writitng; he must return in spirit to the ancient Near East and reach an understanding of the literary forms and styles of the ancient world, none of which is of itself alien to the inspired books (pp. 78-80). Nothing stirs the Fundamentalist to such horror and wrath as the very mention of literary forms and style, which he hates as a detestable diabolical device to destroy the faith of the simple.

Modern interpreters by their use of the researches of history, philology and archaeology have restored confidence in the authority and historical value of the Bible (p.80); the Fundamentalist is convinced that modern biblical study is a direct attack upon the authority and historical value of the Bible. The Holy Father faces the possibility that modern biblical study will produce novel opinions and urges Catholics to receive them with equity, justice and charity, and not with intemperate zeal, reminding Catholics of the wide area of free discussion which the Church leaves to her scholars (p. 82); I shall have to leave it to the Fundamentalist to decide whether his zeal may be at times intemperate.

I scarcely see what can be added to make the repudiation of Fundamentalism more explicit; it is not named, but it is described. The program of current biblical study makes it impossible for anyone to retain Fundamentalism. And — to be practical — scarcely any educated Catholic would now dare to propose Fundamentalism in the extreme form which I have described. It survives among us rather in fear and suspicion of biblical studies, an unwillingness to admit that biblical studies can contribute anything new or rather that they can impose the abandonment of anything old. It survives as a rejection, without examination, of the work of biblical scholars as a firm stand on a "traditional opinion" which will admit of no revision. It is exactly the thinking of the officer of the United States Marines who is going to go right on believing that the Marines were on the shores of Tripoli, no matter what history says.

The Fundamentalist in his distress sometimes calls modern biblical studies a revival of Modernism. Within the space available a thorough refutation of this charge is hardly possible, and one is slightly offended that it should be thought necessary. Most biblical scholars are professors in theological faculties; those who hold this office must begin each year with a public oath that they reject Modernism in the terms of the documents of St. Pius X. Theological studies in the Church are indeed in a bad way if so many of their professors are so dishonest that they casually perjure themselves each year, or so stupid that they cannot recognize Modernism.

But since the word has been carelessly flung about by men who ought to know better, some discussion of the charge is in order for the benefit of those who have not the theological background which would enable them to recognize the charge as false. One who takes the trouble to read modern exegetical literature and to compare it with the works of Modernist writers or with the documents **Lamentabili** (1907) and **Pascendi** (1907) will see at once that he is in two different worlds of thought.

Pius X called Modernism a synthesis of all heresies, and it is difficult to put one's finger on its basic principles, many of which were never candidly expressed by Modernistic writers. I shall essay a somewhat risky description of my own and say that the heart of Modernism is its renunciation of all hope of reconciling faith and reason. The Modernist was the victim of his times; he entered the scene after nearly a century of active literary and historical criticism of the Sacred Scriptures.

To us who now recognize how antiquated much nineteenth-century scholarship has become it is amusing to read confident, even arrogant, writings of men who were sure that many problems were perfectly solved and would never need reconsideration. The Modernist read these writings and was impressed; and he developed the conviction that the educated man simply could not be a believer. He saw the Church losing not only the allegiance but even the respect of the intellectual. Not wishing to renounce his own faith he earnestly sought some way of living both as a believer and as a thinker.

The way he found was to create two worlds of the mind, one ruled by faith and the other by reason. And since logic would not permit two such irreconcilable principles to dwell in the same world, he solved the problem by removing truth from the area of faith. Faith responds to an inner need of man, a need which can be called instinctive or emotional but not intellectual. Faith simply cannot speak the language of the modern educated man, the Modernist believed, and it is a mistake

to conceive of faith as reasonable. It is a paradox
of the human being that he is not a pure mind and
that intellectual satisfaction is not enough; and to
enjoy the satisfaction which faith gives one must
put one's reason in one's pocket. This error, like
most Modernist thinking, was not original; it was
proposed in the thirteenth century by certain
Averroists in a form not substantially different.

Since faith for the Modernist is essentially un-
reasonable, it does not make much difference what
its foundation is. The Modernist therefore regarded
all the statements of her belief made by the Church
as contingent upon the time and place of their
utterance. He found that the primitive thinking
implied in most of them made them intolerable
to the modern thinker as serious utterances intended to communicate something to the mind;
he could accept them only as somewhat inarticulate
cries of a sentiment which he shared with the
Church which uttered the cries.

The Church retained these antiquated formulae,
he thought, only because she had not yet integ-
rated herself with the modern world well enough

to state them in modern language; but even when she did state them, if ever, they could be no more than a different set of inarticulate cries of sentiment. It is the function of the Church, the Modernist would say, to create her own belief without any necessary relation to reality; reality is the area of scholarship. And thus the scholar eliminates all antinomies between faith and reason.

From this basic principle any conclusion can flow, and for this reason the particular propositions of different Modernist writers are less important; the system can go one way or another. It is a synthesis of all heresies because it removes the very principle which makes the idea of heresy possible. There can be no heresy because there are really no articles of faith. The Modernist attitude toward the Bible is not a matter of principles and critical methods, but accepting the Bible as the word of God. Modernists indeed did not deny that the Bible was the word of God, but they did not think that "word" here meant conceptual language.

The controversy concerning the Bible turned on

the historical quality of the Bible. The Modernist understanding of its historical quality was, as I have already observed, determined by literary and historical criticism which is now proved antiquated; and I ought to add by way of parenthesis that Fundamentalism has contributed nothing to this demonstration. In Modernism Christianity ceased to be a historical religion; and since there are only two types of religion, historical and mythological, nothing but mythology was left. This did not distress the Modernist, for man needs religion; and if there is no religion except mythological religion, that is what man must take. It is then only a question of which mythology is superior. The Modernist understood mythology in the old-fashioned sense of nineteenth-century criticism as a misapprehension of reality.

The Modernist and the Fundamentalist positions on the Bible are extremes. Modern biblical scholarship seeks to set itself between the extremes. To the Fundamentalist any movement away from Fundamentalism is a movement in the direction of Modernism, and I suppose he is right; it is a principle of Fundamentalism that no other position is tenable.

But the modern biblical scholar does not feel that he is indebted to Modernism for anything; he is indebted to a body of scholarship which was available to the Modernist and is available to him. He sees no reason why he must make the same mistakes the Modernists did in employing this scholarship, nor does he see why their abuse of learning should be an occasion to forbid all to engage in the pursuit of learning.

The modern biblical scholar is better aware than the general public of the historical character of Judaism and Christianity. Studies of the ancient world bring out the unique quality of Israel and the Church so sharply that it is simply impossible to derive them from the historical and cultural forces of the world in which they arose.

In this sense the modern biblical scholar is more assured of the inbreak of the divine into history than any of his colleagues seem to be. He does not, however — and here he differs from many of them — think that this inbreak can be the object of rigorous historical demonstration; he will say it is demanded by history, which becomes unintelligible without it, but he does not think he can impose the assent of faith upon anyone by historical demonstration.

The idea of the historical quality of the Bible in modern scholarship is not the idea of the Fundamentalist; neither is it that of the Modernist. The modern scholar is convinced that the Bible carries upon its face the marks of a very complex oral and literary tradition. He believes that popular tradition, or folklore, is an adequate vehicle to carry a historical tradition, and he finds it congenial that the tradition of God's word should be borne in the manner proper to men. The manner proper to men does not permit one to lean upon single words and sentences or upon isolated passages, which are meaningful only in the larger context of the Bible.

The modern biblical scholar has been forced to broaden his own idea of history, and he is no longer surprised that the ancients did not think of history as he thinks of it; for he knows that most history in the modern world is folklore too. But he has a great respect for folklore and for history in any form, for it is our sole link with the past from which we come. If he could afford impatience, he would feel it when some completely uninformed journalist sums up the modern biblical movement and its historical criticism as the destruction of the Magi.

The modern biblical scholar hopes that he may have moved toward a solution of the problem which vexed the Modernist — not the reconciliation of faith and reason which, like sin, seems to be a never-ending task, but the reconciliation of faith and history. Where the Modernist made the Faith unhistorical, modern biblical scholarship sees history as a recital of faith. The Bible is salvation history, and we beg to point out that salvation history is history. It is a recital of the saving acts and the judgments of God.

This is its historical value, and it does not make much difference whether the Bible is always and everywhere of uniform quality as an account of external events. Obviously it is not, and obviously also, it is not intended to be. We have found that salvation history can incorporate into itself every type of narrative, prose and poetry, which was known in the ancient world; and we think it is unrealistic to deny without examination that these types can be present.

It is perhaps too early to estimate the fruitfulness of the biblical movement; but enough has happened since 1943 to permit a few observations. The Bible has been brought to the attention of the Catholic public in a way which no one would have thought possible twenty years ago. The purely defensive erudition of Fundamentalism never brought the Bible nearer to priests and laity, and it has shown no new resources.

My own experience and that of my colleagues has been that the public receives modern biblical scholarship with kindness and gratitude; the reception has, of course, been mixed, but it has not been such as to discourage us from continuing our work. If so many people did not attest that this work is serving them, we should have to continue from a sense of duty; but it is easier to continue a work whose value is affirmed.

The favorable attitude of the Holy See, which speaks in these matters through the Pontifical Biblical Commission, has not been altered; it has been reaffirmed since 1943 more than once. In fact this whole development has been magnificently confirmed by the Second Vatican Council in its Dogmatic Constitution on Divine Revelation (Nov. 18, 1965). The movement has gained respect for the Church in many quarters outside her membership, and it has helped Catholics and others to see that one need not be forced to choose between scholarship and faith.

The Biblical Movement and the Laity

Those who have lived with the biblical movement from its beginning look upon it with apprehension which parents feel toward a child who, after a feeble and unpromising childhood, begins to exhibit strength and talent far greater than the strength and talent of his parents. This particular movement began in the midst of a restricted circle of professional biblical scholars and found expression in learned journals and monographs. From these it spread timidly into the classrooms of seminaries, universities and institutes. Then, more secure in its strength and purpose, it moved into other areas of theological study and began to impress its mark upon the clergy. It was a quick and easy step to the laity, both in colleges and universities and through other media of communication. The learned journals and monographs were matched by books and periodical articles addressed to all who were interested, and these

proved to be more numerous than anyone expected. It is safe to say that no theological movement
in the contemporary world has attracted more general interest and impressed more people more
deeply. The biblical movement has found connec-
tions with social studies, liturgical programs and
other activities which, a few years ago, were
scarcely touched by any kind of biblical interpretation.

As the work of scholars, the biblical movement
was international from its beginning. It has re-
mained international, now that it has become popular, and this is a singular witness to its importance. Religious and cultural problems differ sharply from one nation to another, but there is scarcely
any Western country in which the biblical movement is not active and in which it is found irrel-
evant to urgent contemporary questions. In the
United States, publishers and authors have been
surprised by the sale of translations of European
books on the Bible addressed to the general public. It is altogether likely that the traffic will move
both ways in the near future. Such a community of

interest does not appear in all intellectual activities.

The birth of the biblical movement is usually marked as I noted earlier by the encyclical **Divino Afflante Spiritu** of 1943. This is substantially true, but needs qualification. The birth of the United States of America is marked by the Declaration of Independence of 1776, but this event was a climax as much as a beginning. The encyclical conferred the explicit approval of the Holy See upon principles and methods of interpretation which had been formed over a period of twenty years. The document was significant not because it was creative, but because it officially removed restraints upon biblical interpretation never imposed by the Church but imposed by theologians and exegetes themselves as measures of security after the Modernist crises. Statements of the Holy See since 1943 (including the letter to Cardinal Suhard of 1948, the encyclical **Humani Generis** of 1950 and the monitum of the Holy Office of 1961) have encouraged the biblical movement in the direction it has taken. These documents have not, contrary to what some careless readers of them have said, altered or suppressed any existing trend among Catholic interpreters.

Behind the beginnings of the biblical movement are a hundred years of biblical scholarship. Some have wondered at times whether the movement is not a belated acceptance by Catholic scholars of techniques and conclusions worked out in Protestant scholarship. They have questioned whether it is a gain that the Church enrich itself from Protestant learning. Yet one can hardly make the assumption that Protestantism deprives its followers of any intellectual capacity and honesty. Catholic scholars are ready to confess their indebtedness to the work of their Protestant colleagues. It is not widely enough known that Protestant scholars are equally ready to confess their indebtedness to their Catholic colleagues. Contemporary Protestant scholars regard it as narrow to ignore the work of Catholic scholars.

Indeed, the implication that possession of the Catholic faith automatically renders the believer capable of good biblical scholarship is a fallacy.

The Church has the charisma of interpreting the Bible, a charisma which she has exercised with remarkable restraint for two thousand years. No private individual, however, can claim he has this charisma. It is possible to be a devout, even a heroic, Catholic and retain a terrifying number of exegetical errors. Devotion and heroism do not arise from error. By the same token, one should not assume that error does not impose limitations upon devotion and heroism. Ignorance of the word of God does not make one a better Catholic.

The areas of exchange between Catholic and Protestant scholars lie primarily in techniques of criticism and interpretation, in linguistic studies and, most important of all in the study of the history, culture, languages and literature of the ancient Near East. The discovery of the remains of the ancient Near East in the 19th and 20th centuries initiated a Copernican revolution in biblical interpretation. If the study of the history of North America had been conducted for centuries with no knowledge of European history, one can scarcely imagine the difference which the discovery of

European history would have made. The comparison between such a hypothetical discovery and the effect of Oriental studies upon the Bible is not too great an exaggeration. This material is, and remains to this moment, the vital core of the biblical movement. In these studies, confessional differences play little or no part.

The purpose of the biblical movement has been, to borrow a phrase from the Gospels, not to destroy but to fulfill. The scholars who have initiated and carried on the movement have had, as their immediate conscious purpose, the better understanding of the Bible. They were assured that with this better understanding they could more perfectly perform their tasks of teaching the Bible and writing about it.

The desire for a better understanding implies some dissatisfaction with what is often called "traditional interpretation," and scholars are asked why they were dissatisfied with something which had so long satisfied so many. The scholar responds that he knows no reason why biblical interpretation should be the only branch of learning

in which it is a virtue not to advance beyond earlier opinions. He can ask: "What traditional interpretation?" In the context in which this phrase is
used, it is meaningless. "Traditional interpretation"
is a mythological entity, a chimera which has
never existed. The history of biblical interpretation is an area known by very few scholars. It does
seem therefore, that one who wishes to talk about
"traditional interpretation" should have ascer-
tained whether it really exists.

The scholar was dissatisfied with what he had
learned about the Bible — which is not the same
thing as "traditional interpretation" — on several
counts. Twenty-five years ago, the professor of biblical studies taught one of the most neglected and
least respected disciplines in the curriculum. If he
looked outside the academic precincts to the real
world he found that to Catholics, clergy and laity,
the Bible was simply unknown and unimportant at
best, feared and shunned at worst. Many scholars
attributed this condition to the largely defensive
attitude of their predecessors toward the Bible, an
attitude which developed from the panic of the

Modernist crisis. For a generation, Catholic biblical scholarship had concentrated on safety and security — desirable aims surely, but not necessarily achieved only by saying nothing which you have not assured yourself has already been said by a large number of men of proven safety.

In a desire to vitalize their discipline, a number of scholars turned to a body of erudition which had existed long enough to be tested rigorously. Few outside professional circles know how carefully critical and historical studies of the Bible have been purified of the excesses of earlier scholars. Once this material reached students of the Bible, the response was surprising and overwhelming. Scholars found that people desired to share more deeply the understanding which they themselves had gained. Twenty-five years ago, scarcely any Catholic college in the United States had a course in the Bible. I doubt whether there is one today where at least two semesters are not given to the Bible, and if the desires of the teachers and the students are read carefully, the time given to the Bible will be increased rather than shortened.

THE BIBLICAL MOVEMENT AND THE LAITY

Popular acceptance by itself, of course, does not vindicate an intellectual movement. But when so many attest that the biblical movement meets their intellectual and spiritual needs, the fact should not be dismissed lightly.

Why do so many believe that the biblical movement meets their needs? Here in the United States, we are suddenly becoming aware that we have an adult educated laity in large numbers. The existence and purpose of the Catholic intellectual were the object of a vigorous and not always friendly discussion within the last few years. Msgr. John Tracy Ellis noted in the year of his now celebrated article that no member of the American hierarchy was the son of a college graduate. This condition will never recur. In another generation, in all probability, there will be no bishop who is not the son of a college graduate or of college graduates. The implications of this change we have not yet really assessed. But the place of the Bible in the life of the layman, and in particular of the lay intellectual, perhaps can be assessed.

American Catholic higher education has grown

rapidly, at times, like the fastgrowing adolescent boy, awkwardly and disproportionately. While Catholic colleges could easily and quickly achieve respectable positions in the areas of secular learning, they have been faced with the fact that theology is in a long-term period of decline which goes back at least to the 18th century. The reasons for this are too complex and too controversial for discussion here. For the student in Catholic colleges, this has meant that no theological instruction has been available except a condensed and distilled form of the theology which has been taught in seminaries for several generations. Whatever may be the merits of this theology for seminary students, it can be taken as demonstrated that no successful way of adapting it to lay students in Catholic colleges has been discovered and teachers of theology do not expect that a way will be discovered.

In consequence, the Catholic college graduate has matched a genuine and often superior higher education in secular disciplines with a child's knowledge of theology. Since the student was generally neither capable of learning even a summary of seminary theology in the time available, nor was ever greatly interested in learning it, the courses frequently did not differ substantially in form and content from the instruction given in Catholic elementary schools. In the minds of many instructors, the purpose of theology in the colleges was to confirm the students in their Catholic convictions, "to protect their faith." The courses, it was hoped, would enable the students to defend their faith against attacks. Scarcely any one could quarrel with so noble an end; but indoctrination, even when it is directed toward such a lofty object as the faith, remains indoctrination. It is not education.

The remarkable enthusiasm with which teachers of college theology have accepted the work of the biblical movement indicates that, up to this point, it meets their needs and desires better than any other contemporary movement in theology. The systematic theology which has been taught in seminaries is structured on scholastic dialectics, and the American college student has little or no preparation in dialectics. The obstacles which the Bible presents are, indeed, genuine and not always perceived, but at least it does not take one to two years of training in dialectics to remove them. The literary and imaginative character of biblical literature has a certain attraction, once the Bible is recognized as literature and not as a collection of assorted major premises. The Bible is a document of lived experience. These and related features encourage the teacher of theology in the college to believe that this theological course is more accessible to students than any other, although he does not close his eyes to its difficulties.

The response of students to biblical courses has been encouraging in recent years. One must, of course, be careful of claiming success before it is achieved, but results warrant continuing in the same lines. On the other hand, even if such success should be achieved, it can be no more than a temporary stage in progress toward a larger and much more momentous objective.

I have observed above that we have often been

compelled to content ourselves with indoctrination. It has now become apparent that our objective must be the theological education of the laity. The competence which we believe they can attain in secular disciplines must be sought in theology too. This competence is most simply described as the habit of theological thought. Theological thinking has too long been identified with dialectical thinking. One of the contributions of the biblical movement has been to point out that this is too narrow a conception of the habit of theology.

Familiarity with biblical patterns of thought and speech is not the habit of theological thinking either, but it is a necessary component of theological thinking. For it is in biblical language that the truths of our faith have had their earliest and classic expression. One can scarcely study the development of theological understanding without insight into the primitive statements of belief. There is no doubt that familiarity with biblical patterns is within the grasp of the industrious student. Many, for example, have demonstrated their ability to understand the principles of scriptural interpretation.

But if they have acquired this degree of competence, they still will not be endowed with the habit of theology. And here we face an urgent task which contemporary theologians must perform. It is unfortunate that so few have undertaken it. Yet, it is easy to sympathize with their problem. For the task of which I speak demands creative work to a frightening degree.

The task is the creation of the theology of the layman. The word "create" is perhaps too strong, for the elements of the theology of the layman already lie at hand in the Bible and in the Catholic tradition. But they have not been synthesized precisely as a theology of the layman. Theology has been the sicence of the clergy. Conceived within the clerical vocation, it has been concerned with the professional knowledge which prepares the priest to preach and instruct, to hear confessions and administer the other sacraments, to give pastoral counsel and direction. This is not the vocation and mission of the layman. A theological structure with a clerical orientation can never be meaningful to the layman.

The theology of the layman is a theology in the sense that it defines the vocation and mission of the layman in the Church. The layman whose mind is trained in the habit of a theology conceived in terms of his own responsibility will surely be able to exercise the mature judgment in his thinking which we desire him to exhibit in areas of secular learning .

The layman will not be a theological scholar unless he wishes to be. I see no reason why he should not satisfy this desire if he has it. For theological problems touch far more of his personal, professional and public activities than either he or the clergy now realize. An intelligent solution to the immediate problems of the layman is often not possible for the clergy who are, by their calling, removed from full participation in the life of the laity. When they are invoked to solve problems and make decisions which really ought to lie within the personal responsibility of the laity, their solutions and their decisions have not always been wise.

This conception of a theologically educated laity

implies an emancipation of the laity from what some call clerical domination. Without making any judgment about the existing relations between clergy and laity, which differ widely from one country to another, I think we may take it as self-evident that in the Church, as in other societies, the kind of leadership which is demanded for responsible adults who are capable of independent thought and decision is different from the leadership sufficient for a group which is largely uneducated and dependent.

Clerical leadership does not mean clerical control. The finest delicacy of judgment must be shown by those who have the duty of leading. That their task is difficult, and not without danger, is evident. Every parent feels a sense of danger when children reach maturity, and the parents realize that they will no longer make the decision for their children. The conception of a responsible laity may generate some apprehension. But surely, only a responsible laity is able to give a meaning to the term "lay apostolate" — a meaning which the term can never get from a passively docile group which does not move except under total control.

My reflections, it seems, have carried me somewhat beyond the biblical movement. The reflections set forth here, however, have followed the pattern of thinking of many of my colleagues during the last ten years. The impact of modern biblical scholarship has taught us many things. Not the least important of these is the capacity of the layman for sound theological learning. We have found that enough laymen desire this learning to justify serious efforts to communicate it. It has been but a step further to realize the opportunities and responsibilities of the layman who has a genuine education in theology.

We who are engaged in the biblical movement hope sincerely that it will serve the Church. If it is a step toward a fuller and more active participation of the laity in the life and work of the Church, it will have justified itself. Within the area of biblical studies we have learned much, we believe, which makes it easier to join sincere faith with the critical and historical thinking which the modern intellectual world demands.

It is surely no secret that theology has for many years had little to say which was heard by intellectuals either outside the Church or within it. The intellectuals lead the thinking of their communities. This is what they are trained to do and what they are expected to do. The lay intellectual, however, has had less influence on his community as a Catholic than he should have had. We can now hope that this gap between the Church and the world which she must sanctify will be closed. The writings of men like de Lubac, Rahner, Congar, Lonergan, J. Courtney Murray, Gustave Weigel and many others have given us good reason to hope that speculative theology is emerging from its long decline. These men are reaching the lay intellectual whose theological education is nearer than we think.